Francis Frith's
TEIGNMOUTH

Photographic Memories

Francis Frith's
TEIGNMOUTH

Viv Wilson

FRITH
BOOK Co

First published in the United Kingdom in 2002 by
Frith Book Company Ltd

Paperback Edition 2002
ISBN 1-85937-370-4

British Library Cataloguing in Publication Data

Francis Frith's Teignmouth
Viv Wilson

Frith Book Company Ltd
Frith's Barn, Teffont,
Salisbury, Wiltshire SP3 5QP
Tel: +44 (0) 1722 716 376
Email: info@francisfrith.co.uk
www.francisfrith.co.uk

Printed and bound in Great Britain

Front Cover: Teignmouth, Shaldon Beach 1918 68559

AS WITH ANY HISTORICAL DATABASE THE FRITH ARCHIVE IS CONSTANTLY BEING CORRECTED AND IMPROVED
AND THE PUBLISHERS WOULD WELCOME INFORMATION ON OMISSIONS OR INACCURACIES

Contents

FRANCIS FRITH, Victorian founder of the world-famous photographic archive, was a devout Quaker and a highly successful Victorian businessman, philosophic by nature and pioneering in outlook.

By 1855 Francis Frith had already established a wholesale grocery business in Liverpool, and sold it for the astonishing sum of £200,000, which is the equivalent today of over £15,000,000. Now a multi-millionaire, he was able to indulge his passion for travel. As a child he had pored over travel books written by early explorers, and his fancy and imagination had been stirred by family holidays to the sublime mountain regions of Wales and Scotland. 'What a land of spirit-stirring and enriching scenes and places!' he had written. He was to return to these scenes of grandeur in later years to 'recapture the thousands of vivid and tender memories', but with a different purpose. Now in his thirties, and captivated by the new science of photography, Frith set out on a series of pioneering journeys to the Nile regions that occupied him from 1856 until 1860.

INTRIGUE AND ADVENTURE

He took with him on his travels a specially-designed wicker carriage that acted as both dark-room and sleeping chamber. These far-flung journeys were packed with intrigue and adventure. In his life story, written when he was sixty-three, Frith tells of being held captive by bandits, and of fighting 'an awful midnight battle to the very point of surrender with a deadly pack of hungry, wild dogs'. Sporting flowing Arab costume, Frith arrived at Akaba by camel seventy years before Lawrence, where he encountered 'desert princes and rival sheikhs, blazing with jewel-hilted swords'.

During these extraordinary adventures he was assiduously exploring the desert regions bordering the Nile and patiently recording the antiquities and peoples with his camera. He was the first photographer to venture beyond the sixth cataract. Africa was still the mysterious 'Dark Continent', and Stanley and Livingstone's historic meeting was a decade into the future. The conditions for picture taking confound belief. He laboured for hours in his wicker dark-room in the sweltering heat of the desert, while the volatile chemicals fizzed dangerously in their trays. Often he was forced to work in remote tombs and caves where conditions were cooler. Back in London he exhibited his photographs and was 'rapturously cheered' by members of the Royal Society. His reputation as a photographer was made overnight. An eminent modern historian has likened their impact on the population of the time to that on our own generation of the first photographs taken on the surface of the moon.

VENTURE OF A LIFE-TIME

Characteristically, Frith quickly spotted the opportunity to create a new business as a specialist publisher of photographs. He lived in an era of immense and sometimes violent change. For the poor in the early part of Victoria's reign work was a drudge and the hours long, and people had precious little free time to enjoy themselves. Most had no transport other than a cart or gig at their disposal, and had not travelled far beyond the boundaries of their own town or village.

However, by the 1870s, the railways had threaded their way across the country, and Bank Holidays and half-day Saturdays had been made obligatory by Act of Parliament. All of a sudden the ordinary working man and his family were able to enjoy days out and see a little more of the world.

With characteristic business acumen, Francis Frith foresaw that these new tourists would enjoy having souvenirs to commemorate their days out. In 1860 he married Mary Ann Rosling and set out with the intention of photographing every city, town and village in Britain. For the next thirty years he travelled the country by train and by pony and trap, producing fine photographs of seaside resorts and beauty spots that were keenly bought by millions of Victorians. These prints were painstakingly pasted into family albums and pored over during the dark nights of winter, rekindling precious memories of summer excursions.

THE RISE OF FRITH & CO

Frith's studio was soon supplying retail shops all over the country. To meet the demand he gathered about him a small team of photographers, and published the work of independent artist-photographers of the calibre of Roger Fenton and Francis Bedford. In order to gain some understanding of the scale of Frith's business one only has to look at the catalogue issued by Frith & Co in 1886: it runs to some 670 pages, listing not only many thousands of views of the British Isles but

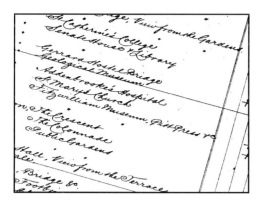

also many photographs of most European countries, and China, Japan, the USA and Canada – note the sample page shown above from the hand-written *Frith & Co* ledgers detailing pictures taken. By 1890 Frith had created the greatest specialist photographic publishing company in the world, with over 2,000 outlets – more than the combined number that Boots and W H Smith have today! The picture on the right shows the *Frith & Co* display board at Ingleton in the Yorkshire Dales. Beautifully constructed with mahogany frame and gilt inserts, it could display up to a dozen local scenes.

POSTCARD BONANZA

The ever-popular holiday postcard we know today took many years to develop. In 1870 the Post Office issued the first plain cards, with a pre-printed stamp on one face. In 1894 they allowed other publishers' cards to be sent through the mail with an attached adhesive halfpenny stamp. Demand grew rapidly, and in 1895 a new size of postcard was permitted called the court card, but there was little room for illustration. In 1899, a year after

Frith's death, a new card measuring 5.5 x 3.5 inches became the standard format, but it was not until 1902 that the divided back came into being, with address and message on one face and a full-size illustration on the other. *Frith & Co* were in the vanguard of postcard development, and Frith's sons Eustace and Cyril continued their father's monumental task, expanding the number of views offered to the public and recording more and more places in Britain, as the coasts and countryside were opened up to mass travel.

Francis Frith died in 1898 at his villa in Cannes, his great project still growing. The archive he created continued in business for another seventy years. By 1970 it contained over a third of a million pictures of 7,000 cities, towns and villages. The massive photographic record Frith has left to us stands as a living monument to a special and very remarkable man.

FRANCIS FRITH's legacy to us today is of immense significance and value, for the magnificent archive of evocative photographs he created provides a unique record of change in 7,000 cities, towns and villages throughout Britain over a century and more. Frith and his fellow studio photographers revisited locations many times down the years to update their views, compiling for us an enthralling and colourful pageant of British life and character.

We tend to think of Frith's sepia views of Britain as nostalgic, for most of us use them to conjure up memories of places in our own lives with which we have family associations. It often makes us forget that to Francis Frith they were records of daily life as it was actually being lived in the cities, towns and villages of his day. The Victorian age was one of great and often bewildering change for ordinary people,

and though the pictures evoke an impression of slower times, life was as busy and hectic as it is today. We are fortunate that Frith was a photographer of the people, dedicated to recording the minutiae of everyday life. For it is this sheer wealth of visual data, the painstaking chronicle of changes in dress, transport, street layouts, buildings, housing, engineering and landscape that captivates us so much today. His remarkable images offer us a powerful link with the past and with the lives of our ancestors.

TODAY'S TECHNOLOGY

Computers have now made it possible for Frith's many thousands of images to be accessed almost instantly. In the Frith archive today, each photograph is carefully 'digitised' then stored on a CD Rom. Frith archivists can locate a single photograph amongst thousands within seconds. Views can be catalogued and sorted under a variety of categories of place and content to the immediate benefit of researchers. Inexpensive reference prints can be created for them at the touch of a mouse button, and a wide range of books and other printed materials assembled and published for a wider, more general readership - in the next twelve months over a hundred Frith local history titles will be published! The day-to-day workings of the archive are very different from how they were in Francis Frith's time: imagine the herculean task of sorting through eleven tons of glass negatives as Frith had to do to locate a particular

See Frith at www. francisfrith.co.uk

sequence of pictures! Yet the archive still prides itself on maintaining the same high standards of excellence laid down by Francis Frith, including the painstaking cataloguing and indexing of every view.

It is curious to reflect on how the internet now allows researchers in America and elsewhere greater instant access to the archive than Frith himself ever enjoyed. Many thousands of individual views can be called up on screen within seconds on one of the Frith internet sites, enabling people living continents away to revisit the streets of their ancestral home town, or view places in Britain where they have enjoyed holidays. Many overseas researchers welcome the chance to view special theme selections, such as transport, sports, costume and ancient monuments.

We are certain that Francis Frith would have heartily approved of these modern developments, for he himself was always working at the very limits of Victorian photographic technology.

THE VALUE OF THE ARCHIVE TODAY

Because of the benefits brought by the computer, Frith's images are increasingly studied by social historians, by researchers into genealogy and ancestory, by architects, town planners, and by teachers and schoolchildren involved in local history projects. In addition, the archive offers every one of us a unique opportunity to examine the places where we and our families have lived and worked down the years. Immensely successful in Frith's own era, the archive is now, a century and more on, entering a new phase of popularity.

THE PAST IN TUNE WITH THE FUTURE

Historians consider the Francis Frith Collection to be of prime national importance. It is the only archive of its kind remaining in private ownership and has been valued at a million pounds. However, this figure is now rapidly increasing as digital technology enables more and more people around the world to enjoy its benefits.

Francis Frith's archive is now housed in an historic timber barn in the beautiful village of Teffont in Wiltshire. Its founder would not recognize the archive office as it is today. In place of the many thousands of dusty boxes containing glass plate negatives and an all-pervading odour of photographic chemicals, there are now ranks of computer screens. He would be amazed to watch his images travelling round the world at unimaginable speeds through network and internet lines.

The archive's future is both bright and exciting. Francis Frith, with his unshakeable belief in making photographs available to the greatest number of people, would undoubtedly approve of what is being done today with his lifetime's work. His photographs, depicting our shared past, are now bringing pleasure and enlightenment to millions around the world a century and more after his death.

In the year 2000, a small group of people gathered on Teignmouth's river beach to remove a wooden structure from the end of a line of beach huts. This was one of England's last remaining bathing machines. Few watched its removal for specialist renovation, but many will appreciate its presence in the proposed extension at Teignmouth Museum.

When touchstones such as this are elevated by preservation, it sometimes kindles fresh interest in local history. The bathing machine's fabric - a blistered skin of azure blue paint covers pitch pine walls beneath a rounded roof - is saturated with the sights, sounds and smells of

Teignmouth, From Torquay Rd 1924 76375

the seaside, fermented by years of innocent delight in coastal sojourns. I regard the machine as the last witness to the resort's glory days, a solitary remnant embodying the spirit of the past. On the following pages, with the help of Frith's photographers, we will now look back to a golden era when coast was king, and

Teignmouth was a resort enjoyed as much by those on Sunday School outings as well-to-do families renting sunny villas.

Yet in looking back over the centuries, we also encounter the history of Teignmouth's harbour and its role in feeding the town's inhabitants. We must also look inland to farming in the surrounding countryside: the market route used to lead steeply up over Haldon and down the deep lanes to Exeter. One foot on the deck and one hand on the plough, so were the men of Devon, and vestiges of an agricultural age can still be found in Teignmouth's hinterland.

Later, transport and tourism developed in tandem. The new railway brought a sudden influx of visitors and scores more poured in from pleasure steamers. Others came by motorbike, car and charabanc, and in their wake came air-borne passengers from Haldon

Bottom Left:
Teignmouth, From Torquay Rd 1890 26021

Top Right:
Teignmouth, 1911 63693

Bottom Right:
Teignmouth, From Torquay Rd 1924 76375

Teignmouth is spread out map-like before its beholder, revealing its dual profiles of working harbour and seafront showplace. In 1890, the New Quay of 1821 protrudes from the river beach, sweeping in front of properties lining Teign Street. In 1911, sailing dinghies suggest that it is Regatta Week. A steam tug is moored at the foot of Ivy Lane and beach tents pepper the sands near the pier with its fine new ballroom at the seaward end. In the 1920s, rubble dumped on the Point was covered with a layer of concrete to provide a car park beside Lifeboat House. The Singers' Pavilion straddles the sea wall beyond the lighthouse of 1845.

Top Left:
Detail of the pier
Teignmouth, From Torquay Rd 1890 26021

Bottom Left:
Detail of the steam tug
Teignmouth, From Torquay Rd 1890 26021

Bottom Right:
Detail of the beach tents
which pepper the sands near the pier
Teignmouth 1911 63693

Aerodrome. The bittersweet years sandwiched between two World Wars ushered in the highs and lows of shifting fashion and fortune.

Frith's high-quality photographs provide a stunning visual record of Teignmouth between 1890 and 1965. Two or three images recorded from approximately the same place but separated by several years allow intriguing comparisons, and the dating of local features with reasonable accuracy. Through this unique record, interest and knowledge of Teignmouth's past may reach new heights.

Invading Danes are believed to have sailed up the river, only to be induced into concord at Bishopsteignton's Peace Field. In 1044, Edward the Confessor granted parcels of land to Bishop Leofric of Crediton. Church ownership influenced development; by the 14th century the port had an expanding trade in fish and salt. It attracted the attentions of the French and was damaged by them in 1340. Six years later the Black Death snatched a third of the town's inhabitants and after the second French invasion of 1690, the town was left in smoking ruins.

It is not easy to picture the town struggling to overcome the after-effects of a short-lived but destructive invasion. Its core was a marsh crossed by several bridges. Considering their water supply was dipped from streams and wells, the inhabitants of the town's 3-400 houses were surprisingly healthy.

The Battle of Waterloo in 1815 quenched the fear of invasion from the French and sig-

Teignmouth, St Michael's Church 1911 63701
St Michael's stands on one of the oldest religious sites in Devon. In 1887, a new tower and western walls, costing £2,500, were built to commemorate Queen Victoria's Golden Jubilee. An unusual feature is the bench with gates in the boundary wall.

Top Right: **Teignmouth, Roman Catholic Church 1906** 56568

South Devon Railway purchased the first Catholic Church of 1854 for £2000 after deciding to open the railway tunnels beneath it. After piecemeal dismantling, it was re-erected as the Church of the Holy Cross in east Plymouth. The church of Our Lady and St Patrick was built higher up the hill on the site of Eastcliff House stables in 1880.

Bottom: **Teignmouth, Congregational Church 1906** 56569

A tour of Tuscany may have inspired the London architect Sulman, engaged in the 1880s to design the church. He exceeded the £4,300 budget by £600. The spire on the right was later removed. In the 1700s, a bridge spanned the Litterbourne, a deep ditch that ran down the hill and into Mere Lane on the right, below the cobbled pavement.

nalled an optimistic era, pushing the craze for building to new heights. Several significant houses with sizeable grounds date from the decade following victory. The Duke of Somerset who owned the New Quay, spent the winter of 1833 in Courtenay Terrace, the first of the impressive rows to be constructed on the Den. Bitton Estate was large enough to include three prominent dwellings and spacious grounds for archery competitions. Yarmouth MP, Winthrop Mackworth Praed who established the Boys' Library at Eton College, grew up at Bitton. Praed was a poet and attended services at West Teignmouth Parish Church with "his hair brushed into a tuft on either side and a velvet collar turned down over his coat". Bitton's most illustrious occupant was Sir Edward Pellew who became Lord Exmouth. The exploits of this Admiral of the Blue inspired Forester's fictional character Horatio Hornblower.

The town we see today began emerging during the 19th century. Fines were imposed on anyone caught emptying a chamber pot in the gutter other than between midnight and five in the morning. A scavenger removed 'night soil' and cleaned the streets. Teignmouth's Improvement Act of 1836 promoted a reliable domestic supply of water and gas. Six churches and three chapels ensured that the religious revival of the 19th century was not overlooked. The unavoidable human affairs of hatching, matching and despatching in places of worship included a local custom of ringing a Passing Bell. The moment breath left a body, someone was sent to pay the Sexton one shilling to ring it for 15 minutes. A few seconds interval separated each toll, one for a man, two for a woman and three for a child.

Weekly markets and annual fairs sustained the needs of the population, increased by adventurous visitors arriving by water conveyance or horse-drawn stagecoach. Frequent flooding of the marshland was endured until extensive reclamation took place in the late 1700s. Primitive dipping places were banished and the marshes drained. The river Tame dividing the town was taken underground and the level of the town centre raised. Man's best endeavours were nevertheless thwarted by a fateful cocktail of heavy rainfall and high tide on several occasions. A flood in 1859 caused closure of the railway line for two days while rapid repairs were effected by one thousand workers. The 'Great Deluge' of 1875 transformed the town into a Venice without gondolas. Another storm in 1894 impeded through-passage for trains, raised great slabs of paving stones in Brook Street and flooded shop cellars, which were pumped out between tides.

Opportunities to build on reclaimed land brought a wave of optimism and the new town blossomed with churches, theatres, libraries and shops. The gulf separating rich and poor is illustrated through comparison between the wellborn who sent barrels of Teign oysters to their friends via the railway and the needy who relied on charity for survival. The Soup Kitchen kept poor families fed and the Blanket Society kept them warm. Over 600 blankets were loaned out during the winter of 1895. Many a conscience was salved through the conveyance of a charitable deed. The earliest forms of education were funded by the purses of the wealthy and the gulf reduced through a local trade in baskets, barrels, hats, musical instruments, saddles, silver, sails - even the making of wheels and coaches.

The Town Crier broadcast news and posted bills and the streets were filled with music from the hurdy-gurdy, mobile piano or wind-up gramophone on a trolley. Street hawkers sold paper hats and windmills, baskets of watercress and fish and chips.

Local growth was not hindered by economic recession elsewhere and a noteworthy Town Hall,

Teignmouth, Regent St 1906 54060

It is surprising that the fruit stores and café on the left continue the same trade at the start of the 21st century! The trio of gas globes contrast with the more up-to-date version next to the cabmen's shelter on the edge of the Triangle's railed garden. On the left we can see a three-wheeled delivery cart with wicker basket.

market and fire station were opened in 1883.

Responsibility for improvements to the twin parishes of the 19th century town lay with the Local Government Board formed in 1859. Its evolution to Teignmouth Urban District Council in 1894 coincided with the expansion of the harbour and railway network. Statistics reveal that the town's population almost doubled from 3,980 in 1821 to 6,013 in 1868.

Shaldon's sloping hillside grants exceptional overviews of Teignmouth and its sheltered harbour tucked into the river's final bend. A wider panorama embraces the coastline stretched into a diminishing border of dark amber. The Teign, an artery rising on Dartmoor's upland, divides the favoured resort of Teignmouth from cherished Shaldon. Vital links between the two were initiated through an 11th century ferry crossing and further extended by a bridge in the 19th century.

After the second French invasion of 1690, the town was left in smoking ruins. A period of extensive development followed, during which a new Teignmouth emerged as a high-class watering place. The gentry took prolonged sojourns amidst the splendour of fine residences, hotels, clubs and assembly rooms. Happily, much of the architecture has survived and out-numbers the grotesque structures of the post-war period. Shaldon graduated along a similar route to its larger neighbour, and the village blossoms with architectural gems of the Regency period.

The harbour generated many local livelihoods before the holiday trade evolved. In the early days, before the advent of larger scale commercial fishing, local inhabitants kept the wolf from the door by harvesting shellfish, mackerel and herring. In 1880, local fishing boats numbered 305, keeping 118 men and boys at work. Their catch was loaded into wooden barrels, hauled by horses to the railway station and sent to Billingsgate Market. Winter night fishing for herring had few joys. Boats worked as a group, the crew setting out nets with corks and buoys and lead-weighted footlines. Lanterns were lit and the fishermen sang to while away the hours until a shoal

drifted into the nets. One hand on the oar kept the boat broadside while the other hauled in the catch. An article of 1875 says: 'Those who think the herring dear at one penny each should go out a few hours drifting. The danger is very great. Shortly after we came in, Cox's boat stuck on the bar and went to pieces. Since then, one of the boats has been overturned and two of the crew drowned.'

When the March to September licence to

Teignmouth
The Pier and Ness House
c1955 T21058

Bottom Left:
Detail of World War Two gun base

Bottom Right:
Detail of Ness House

The Cliffords, Lords of the Manor of West Teignmouth, owned the Regency gem of Ness House for about six generations. Early in the 20th century it belonged to shipping magnates called Holder, who may have created the first so-called Smugglers' Tunnel leading to a private beach on the far side of Ness headland. Ornamental gardens with a fishpond were laid and public access granted after Devon County Council purchased the grounds in 1949. Ness House became a hotel and was enlarged in recent years. On the left of this image is a large World War Two gun base.

fish for salmon in the river cost £5, wholesale prices for a pound ranged between 8d and two shillings (10p). Some salmon weighed over 50 pounds and had the strength to knock a man over and leap overboard. If a shark or monkfish tore the seine nets to shreds, it was sometimes strapped to a barrow and pushed through town as a curiosity in the hope of raising a few coppers to defray expenses. In the estuary, flat fish were speared with fluking irons and down at Red Rock, Mother Boone is recalled tucking her skirts into her bloomers and wading into the mud to pin down enough for a meal!

Teignmouth, From Shaldon c1965 T21095

Some local people still remember the spine-chilling sight of bomb-carrying enemy aircraft racing up the estuary. The district suffered 22 air raids.

Today, the estuary abounds with watercraft of all kinds yet those who seek to linger in the past discover that a ferry ride across to Shaldon on a warm and sunny day is a true transport of delight.

A dry ski slope was laid on Ness slopes in the 1960s and was itself supplanted by the Approach Golf Course.

Today, some residents can still remember Mr Nathan selling fresh fish from a handcart and Mrs Belton serving winkles in paper cones from her tattered pram loaded with shellfish. And not forgetting the pasty man who marched about with a steaming tray of toothsome savouries, yelling 'All 'ot!'

Some inhabitants teetered above subsistence level by dealing in contraband tobacco and liquor. The risk of being hung or shot failed to deter the smugglers, pursued by patrols of gun-carrying men until the formation of the Coastguard Service in 1822. Smuggling has never completely died out in this region. Safer livings were gained beyond river and sea when commercial growth provided jobs in hotels, houses, shops, clubs and banks. Many women took in washing and squeezed their family into one room to vacate

Teignmouth, Shaldon Bridge 1922 73092

The cost of the wooden bridge of 1827 was £20,000. Claimed to be the longest in England at 1,671 feet, it had 34 arches and a swing bridge allowing passage for tall-masted ships. Two major collapses in the 19th century led to a new bridge of reinforced concrete and steel, completed in 1931. Devon County Council abolished tolls in 1948 after purchasing the bridge for £90,000. Major strengthening works were done in 2001/2002 The toll board, left of the gate, is now on display in Teignmouth Museum.

The drover's tunnel next to Shaldon Bridge was a perfect example of agricultural archaeology until major works in the 1990s involved the installation of a huge pipe that stole half the tunnel's width. None-the-less, try to imagine farmers driving their cattle, fat from lush grasslands south of the river, through the shallows and into the tunnel beneath the railway line.

beds for paying guests in summer.

The harbour was at its commercial liveliest in the 19th century. Six boat building yards along the banks of the Teign turned out vessels of 3-400 tons. Rope and sailmakers were kept busy close by. Flax or cotton was used to make the sails that were boiled in cauldrons of red dye obtained from oak tree bark.

Daily market boats going upriver to Newton Abbot passed heavily laden flat-bottomed lighters from the canals of Stover and Hackney. Loads of clay or granite were transferred in the harbour to sea-going ships. 'Lumpers' used spiked sticks to handle Kingsteignton ball clay, cut into 10 inch cubes. The clay trade, which had its infancy in the 18th century, continues to thrive.

Unruly behaviour by lightermen led to calls for prohibition of their beer allowance. Victorian Temperance worker, Miss Caroline Fry brought an action in the police court on the grounds that the allowance contravened the Truck Act. She lost the case but opened a shelter for lightermen on the river beach, curiously enough, next door to the Jolly Sailor Inn!

The harbour's commercial growth increased after gaining independence from the port of Exeter in 1852. An optimist predicted that future imports and exports would be counted in thousands of tons through 'Industry, Perseverance and Independence'

Bottom Left:

Teignmouth, View up the River Teign from Ness c1960 T21062

Compare this with earlier photographs to see the development of the car park at the Point. The lighthouse of 1953 is a memorial to Philip Lucette. Rising ground near the bridge shows Mill Lane houses on the right and post-war prefabricated bungalows on the left. Two large cylindrical holders mark the site of the gas works at Broadmeadow.

Bottom Right:

Teignmouth, From Shaldon 1924 76388

We can still enjoy a network of narrow lanes that snake through Shaldon's delightful hotch-potch of architectural styles. Not long after this photograph was taken, a new hospital was built on the rural fieldscape across the river. In the foreground, we can see the village green.

**Shaldon
Beach 1918** 68559

Shaldon House
stands majestically
beyond a pair of tall
gateposts. The gate
preserved the priva-
cy of the Ness head-
land until the County
Council purchased it
in 1949. Bay
Cottage, which we
can just glimpse
with its distinctive
roofline and seclud-
ed summerhouse on
the wooded hillside
above, belonged to
Ivy Carus Wilson
who married the
renowned boat
builder FC Morgan
Giles.

but it took a century to achieve. Zinc, lead and manganese won from nearby mines and quarries added to the export trade. Building materials, coal and a vast assortment of commodities required by inhabitants and visitors accounted for increasing imports. Towards the

Teignmouth, Boarding the Ferry 1922 73086

River Teign ferry dues were part of the Duke of Cornwall's perquisites in the 11th century.
The ferry rights, acquired by the Lord of West Teignmouth Manor, Lord Clifford, were sold to
the Bridge Company in 1827. The fare in the 1920s was one penny or a penny h'penny return.

Teignmouth, The Harbour c1965 T21091
Inadequate store sheds recorded here were swept away in a massive upheaval of the harbour in the 1980s, driving port trade to new heights. Morgan Giles' Shipyard produced pleasure craft and coastal defence vessels in several buildings on the right between 1920 and 1964. Twenty five years after closure, waterside apartments were built on the site and public access to the entire length of the river beach restored after 60 years closure. On the right, we can see the 'Big Shed' at Morgan Giles' Shipyard.

end of the 1800s, the harbour handled about 125,000 tons each year.

The docks were updated but as the 20th century dawned, trade was erratic and survival was in the balance for several decades. In the 1940s, the restoration of normal conditions marked a fresh start. Clay was the main export and the workforce of about 500 witnessed the eclipse of vessels of 700 tons by ships twice that size. Constant dredging of shifting sandbanks became necessary to ensure access for the new breed of ships. Growth was spurred on by the 1980s closure of Exmouth Docks; currently the annual average is around 620,000 tons through some 500 ships that serve most countries of the European Union. Teignmouth Quay Company was sold to Associated British Ports in 1987 and entered the 21st century on a wave of optimism.

Teignmouth was the second location in 18th century Devon to gain favour as a resort for the upper classes. First the gentry, preoccupied by the fear of illness and disease, came in pursuit of improved health. Yet accommodation was in short supply until Teignmouth's marshy central core was drained, allowing extensive and tasteful development on reclaimed ground. Large boarding houses, inns, hotels and shops quickly grew out of the mud. Even when cholera was raging through England, the local newspaper observed that: 'Teignmouth is like an arc of peace in the midst of a deluge of pestilence, affording refuge to hundreds driven from their homes'.

Top Right: **Detail of Teignmouth, 1906** 56562
Top Left: **Detail of Teignmouth, Beach 1896** 37606
Bottom Right: **Detail of Teignmouth, New Parade 1910** 62449
Bottom Left: **Detail of Teignmouth, sands from Pier 1931** 84013

Teignmouth, Beach 1896 37606
This photograph shows the male bathers' beach with orange and blue painted bathing machines.
Between the buildings on the shore, masts of sailing ships at the end of Ivy Lane can be glimpsed.

Above: **Teignmouth, 1906** 56562

In this later image, suits and towels hired by male bathers hang out to dry. The top of the sea wall provides additional seating and a pagoda shelter adorns the promenade. Transient diversions on the far side of the Den have attracted a group of onlookers.

Right: **Teignmouth, Parade 1910** 62452

By 1910, the Singers' Pavilion has been added - visible beyond the bathing machines - along with a hand-turned roundabout with ponies and swing boats. A row of winches for bathing machines line the sands. A small screen protects plants in the nearest bed from south-westerly winds.

Visitors began to drink seawater as a cure. If the results can be believed, the practice was miraculous! Hysterical ladies were restored to normal spirits, cripples were able to walk and lepers were cleansed. The craze for bathing in it gained impetus through the invention of bathing machines. The resort had 16 when the poet John Keats brought his ailing brother here in 1818. Six years later Lady Harriet Silvester's diary recorded that Teignmouth was 'a small place originally, but much increased by lodging houses and libraries, ballrooms etc. The shore is remarkably good for bathing'. The spectacle of the annual regatta pleased her Ladyship's eye and she

Below: Teignmouth, Sands from Pier 1931 84013

In 1931, it's out with bathing machines and in with huts and tents. The sea has snatched the Singers' Pavilion and the promenade is now adorned with new shelters, bandstand and the war memorial of 1922.

records meeting the renowned artist, Thomas Luny. Meanwhile, a son of Teignmouth, Elias Parish was gaining a rapturous following as the 'prodigious English Harpist', according to Berlioz in 1842.

The reputation of Tingmouth, as it was known locally, was increased by satisfied visitors broadcasting news of its equable climate with mild winters and above average hours of sunshine. The beach to the east of the pier remained exclusive to female bathers who were rolled into the shallows in modesty-preserving bathing machines. Out they stepped, gowned from neck to toe in a thick dark mate-

Top Left: **Teignmouth, The Beach and Pier c1960** T21067

By the 1960s, the glory days of the pier were coming to an end, with few of the talent competitions, fashion parades, afternoon tea dances, charity balls and gala dinners of late 1940s and 50s.

The following photographs taken from the pier benefit from close comparison.

Bottom Left: **Teignmouth, From the Pier 1903** 49563

Top Right: **Teignmouth, New Parade 1910** 62449

In 1903, Regency and Victorian buildings blend harmoniously. The prominent central buildings were the hotels of Berkeley and Esplanade. Adverts for Pears soap are displayed on some of the 18 bathing machines. By 1910, about £15,000 had been spent repairing the sea wall and pier after a storm in January 1908. The lower level prom has new benches.

rial. Attached to the machine was a rope with a cork on the end; the ladies clung to this as they bobbed about in the waves and indulged in a great deal of screaming.

In 1901, the vicar of St Michael's asked the council to prevent the unseemly spectacle of 'indecent bathing near the church' on Sunday mornings. Byelaws affecting bathing machines were adjusted after a man drowned from lighthouse beach in the 1920s, when family bathing was permitted but only before eight in the morning. Bathing machines gave way to tents and then to timber beach huts. Every opportunity to extract cash from visitors was exploited through the sale of tea, ice cream and shellfish and pleasure boats trips. Some people scratched a living from concert parties at the open-air pavilion on the sea wall. Two hand-turned roundabouts operated

Top:
**Teignmouth, From Pier
1911** 63697

Bottom Left:
**Teignmouth, From Pier
1922** 73078

**By 1911, Punch and Judy
shows were an essential
element of seaside
holidays. The booth with
its striped canopy was
moved between
locations by the small
handcart upended at the
rear. Hoards of
workers from Midland
Factories, Fry's of Bristol
and Swindon-based
railwaymen and their
families were choosing
Teignmouth for their
annual holidays. Bathing
machines total 26.**

Teignmouth, 1925 78461
Bathing machines are still in use in 1925. Trips round the bay and along the coast or up the river in local-built pleasure boats provide summer incomes for many local families.

on the sand and crowds of children rallied for Punch and Judy shows and hymn-singing Sunshine Hour.

Teignmouth's Swimming and Lifesaving Society included several county champions who regularly swam from the pier to Babbacombe. Hundreds of spectators packed pleasure boats and the shoreline to watch races and water polo matches. Lifeboat Day was another eagerly awaited spectacle. The crew rowed out to the end of the pier, pulled on ropes attached to the gunwhales and turned the heavy lifeboat upside down. The circle was completed almost immediately and the vessel self-righted to the sound of hearty cheering from the crowd. The manoeuvre was generally repeated six times.

The years rolled by in a familiar pattern: deck chair attendants trudged through the sand with ticket rolls and heavy leather cash bags, children cried over spilt ice creams and grandparents bemoaned the sand in their sandwiches. Yet changing tastes gradually crept in, although few anticipated the demise of the town's tourist-based livelihoods. When in the 1960s the majority were lured away to hotter climes through cheap package tours, Teignmouth began to feel the pinch and its character changed. It was the end of an era.

Teignmouth
The Promenade from the Pier c1960 T21047
Plans for the Normandy landings in 1944 were discussed at Courtenay House on the left of the terrace. Front gardens have now given way to parking spaces. Sun decks and the wishing well in a sunken garden on the prom have since been removed. Meanwhile, a circular pavilion once planned for the bombed-site at Esplanade has failed to materialise.

The Teignmouth Journal of 1893 illuminates the ancient Den, Dune or Dene: 'The Dene is a Saxon word for sandy waste. As the Point is now, so was the whole of the Den and the ground occupied by Powderham Terrace. The fine sand left to the mercy of the wind drifted into hillocks, consequently the surface was so undulating that a man walking across it would be completely lost from view as he sank into one of the deep gullies.'

The plan of 1805 shows an outline of buildings planned by Courtenay, Lord of the Manor of East Teignmouth. The north end of the terrace bearing his family name is already complete. A windmill and a fort against the French stood near a hillock close to the site where the lighthouse was built in 1845. Nearby, there was a grandstand for the upper classes to witness a host of activities including wrestling and cricket. Boys from Eton School played a match on the Den in 1814. Races were staged between horses, donkeys and even pigs! Almost every backyard had its own hog for fattening and they were press-ganged into racing across the Den for visitors' amusement. When cycling became fashionable in the 1880s, races of varying lengths took place.

The Local Board bought the Den from Lord Courtenay in 1869. The undulating dunes were levelled and a carriageway and promenade laid using thousands of tons of soil from the development of Orchard Gardens. When Mill Lane and Bishopsteignton Rd were creat-

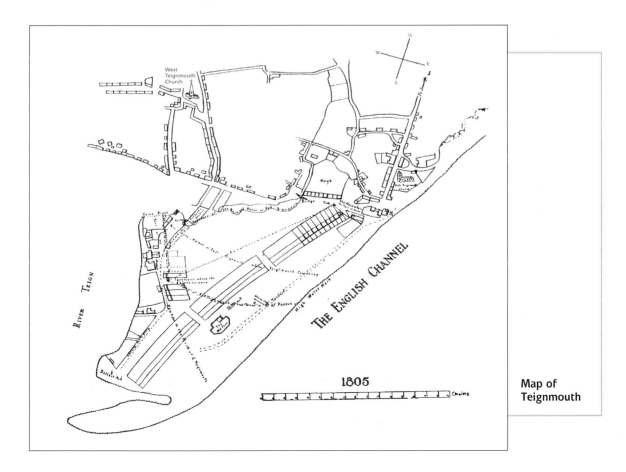

1805

Map of
Teignmouth

ed in 1912, more soil was transferred to the Den to make banks and rockeries. The Local Board had an obligation to allow recreational use 'equally for all classes', but they tried to protect their investment in the Den by asking the police to enforce their edict of 1875: 'Cricket, football, rounders and other games and amusements that interfere with or cause damage to the general public are strictly forbidden. Proceedings will be taken against all guilty of infringement or of improper language on highways adjoining'.

In the same year, the favoured spectacle of drill practise was not as polished as might be expected: 'They did a march-past in open and closed columns in quick time and at the double and practised numerous evolutions in 90 minutes. It was not satisfactory, many men moving in a slovenly fashion throwing their company out of order'.

Military visits attracted huge crowds eager for the excitement of the firing of small guns, the playing of bands and a colourful firework finale. The Devon Yeomen in red jackets and busbies were firm favourites. In 1892, hundreds of people, determined not to miss out on the sight of parading Yeoman, travelled in by cart, coach and four, bicycle, pleasure steamer and tug when the railway was closed for 31 hours to allow the broad gauge rails to be narrowed.

Teignmouth Urban District Council (TUDC) replaced the Local Board in 1894. Numerous complaints of bad behaviour on the Den were recorded. At the Petty Sessions of 1900, fines were imposed for 'furiously riding a pony' and for being drunk and disorderly. An Inspector of Nuisances was paid £60 a year to impose strict control and record the names of offenders. A new bowling green spurred local objection. William Gilpin considered it misappropriation of public space and continued to exercise his right of access by crossing the green daily in

hob-nail boots.

The gentry promenaded in their finery across the Den, adding to the leisurely weaving of a vivid tapestry of public celebrations, carnivals and fetes. The annual visit of the funfair with its rattling trucks and steaming tractors signalled local children to rally for every motion of its fascinating assembly. People indulged in pony or donkey rides or took drives in a bath chair or invalid carriage. All age groups revelled in skipping days when

extra long ropes allowed the masses to skip in unison. Games of living chess were played on a giant board. Children dressed as black and white chess pieces obeyed moves called by schoolmasters perched on lofty umpire chairs.

Much of the elegant architecture of the buildings overlooking the Den is attributed to Andrew Patey from Exeter. The Assembly Rooms of 1826, celebrating Sir Edward Pellew's advancement to Admiral after the successful bombardment of Algiers ten years

Teignmouth
Bowling Green 1907 58125A

A game of bowls cost 2d per hour in the green's maiden season of 1907. The pier of 1867 cost £8,000 to build. This entrance replaced the original destroyed by a storm in 1908.

earlier, cost £2000. The cash was raised through £5 shares held by Lord Courtenay and forty stakeholders. The Ionic portico above a Doric colonnade suggests inspiration from the finest of Grecian styles. The ground floor was for dressing rooms, stewards' apartments, billiards and reading rooms. A grand staircase led up to the terrace, ballroom, and rooms for tea and card playing. Teignmouth & East Devon Club occupied it from 1890 to 1908 when the delights of a champagne supper could be had for one guinea.

The new owner, restaurateur Charles Sayce, converted it to the Riviera Hotel. Its use as a cinema with a hand-operated cinemagraph dates to Easter 1912 when the ballroom with 350 seats was leased to Poole's Perfect Pictures. Bill Prince paid £2,500 for the Riviera in 1924 and a decade later invested £33,000 on a deco style auditorium for 900. New equipment included one of the biggest screens in the area, its 470 square feet framed within a proscenium 45 foot wide. The 1960s brought horizontal division with an amusement arcade at street level. The cinema closed in 2000 and its future currently hangs in the balance.

Above: **Teignmouth, Bowling Green 1930** 83255

The weather station, surrounded by the white fence, has recorded temperatures and hours of sunshine since 1905. Information is relayed to local and national newspapers. Teignmouth claims to be one of the sunniest spots in England. Yet in 1930, the newly opened Den Pavilion had just had an unprofitable first season.

Opposite: **Teignmouth, 1924** 76376

A solitary motor car parked beside Den Crescent portends a new age of travel. Trees have been planted along the Den's border in front of the Royal Hotel. About 2000 visitors could be accommodated in the seafront hotels between the wars.

Below: **Teignmouth, The Den 1936** 87486

The Assembly Rooms of 1826 had a ballroom, library, billiards, cards and social rooms for the gentry. It became an exclusive club then a hotel. The first moving pictures were projected in the ballroom in 1912. This photograph records it soon after massive internal upgrading to a 1930s deco super-cinema.

Opposite: **Teignmouth, Den looking south 1890** 26038

Below: **Teignmouth, Parade 1910** 62451

Courtenay Terrace replaced a row of two-storey cottages in the 1800s. Council benches were made of lasting materials, giving over a century of service.

In the 18th century, a single gun battery stood in the foreground and the area has since been referred to as The Gun. In the later photograph (62451), labourers can be seen carrying out improvements to the road surface.

Gentle curves of the Den's twin crescents of 1825 were perfectly complimented by Cockram's Coaching House, renamed the Royal Hotel soon after its inception. Patronage included Queen Maria Amelia and her three children following Louis Philip's abdication. Bed and breakfast was three shillings in the early days. The hotel was extended by a third floor in the 1930s. UK and American troops commandeered it during the war. President Eisenhower and Winston Churchill are said to have planned their strategy within its walls. The Visitors' Book recorded many celebrities, including The Beatles, who attracted great excitement in the 1960s when the Royal's final days as the town's social centrepiece were drawing to a close. New Year's Eve was a never-to-be-forgotten event. The band played 'Scotland the Brave' as the head chef paraded around the ballroom, arms out-stretched bearing a huge silver salver of flaming Christmas pudding. The author witnessed every stage of the building's prolonged demolition, ending with the majestic portico on All Fools' Day 1998. It was replaced by Royal Court.

TUDC secured a loan of £3,450 from the Minister of Health to build an architectural misfit of iron and glass. The Den Pavilion was opened in June 1930. No less than 885 seats were selected in three qualities: 190 velvet-covered front of theatre seats budgeted at 27/6 (£1.38) each; 238 middle seats at 23/6 (£1.17) each; and 457 rexine-covered rear seats at 10/6 (55p) each. Teignmouth Electric Lighting Company was paid £130.7s to install lights. TUDC borrowed another £1,800 to complete the Pavilion. However, the first season was not successful. Subsequently the Licencee financed alterations, moving the stage to its current position at the seaward end. TUDC extended the lease by ten years and reduced the rent from £350 to £300 per annum.

In 1943, American troops used the Pavilion as a canteen served from a nissen hut cook-house on an open site where the bowling club-house now stands. Leaks in the roof forced 1950s theatre-goers to use umbrellas during performances. A massive upgrading took place in 1967 when it was renamed the Carlton Theatre. The Teignmouth Players amateur group took over its lease in 1984.

Opposite: **Teignmouth, Tennis Courts 1922** 73087

Below: **Teignmouth, Tennis Courts 1936** 87485

The tennis courts date from 1910, when it cost 4d (2p) to hire a court and balls for an hour. The tall bay-windowed property on the left housed Lendrick, a private academy for boys. The Royal Hotel charged 63 shillings (£3.15) for a week's stay between the wars.

By 1936 a miniature putting green has been added. The Royal Hotel roofline depicts vertical growth with an extra floor added to the right-hand end. The other wing was similarly developed, unbalancing the original design. Motor cars and telegraph wires indicate the growth of transport and communications.

Opposite: **Teignmouth, The Den 1911** 63699

Before the construction of Powderham Terrace in the 1860s, fishermen dried and repaired nets close to their humble cottages on the Den. By 1840, a piped water supply and gas lighting were available to each household in the town and the streets were cleaned daily by a scavenger.

Below: **Teignmouth, Lynton House c1960** T21501

Ten people were killed when a bomb fell on numbers 4, 5 and 6 Powderham Terrace on Sunday 10th January, 1943. A space existed for several years beside number 7, Lynton House, one of the few remaining seafront hotels in the 21st century.

Teignmouth, The Terrace Walk 1911 63698
Old Maids' Walk or Perch at Eastcliff gained curiosity value early in the 20th century when arches of whale jawbones were raised at both ends.

Nineteenth century visitors enjoyed the benefits of progress through the construction of the promenade and the new sea wall. The Local Government Board carried out improvements to the seafront and Den following piece-meal purchase of the manor of east Teignmouth. Early photographs illustrate the new defensive wall, intended to reduce the risk of flooding in the low-lying town centre. The sea challenged the wall's strength on numerous occasions and succeeded in breaching it in 1890 and again in January 1908, when a momentous storm caused £15,000 worth of damage to the wall and decorative pagodas at the pier's entrance.

Old Maid's Walk at Eastcliff became a landmark when arches of whale jawbones were erected at both ends. Mr Pike Ward, local shipbroker and founder director of Teignmouth Quay Company, brought the bones from Iceland. He was a much respected fish dealer and became Vice Consul for

Norway and Sweden. Small fish rejected by Icelanders were brought to Teignmouth in Pike Ward's boat Elise. In 1900, 100 tons were brought in for local consumption.

Over 20 ships were wrecked in the bay between 1850 and 1917. A contemporary sign near the Yacht Club HQ explains the legal protection of Church Rocks Wreck, which was discovered by local teenager Simon Burton during a snorkling expedition in 1975. A significant bronze cannon lifted from the site led to years of serious archaeological excavation, revealing the scant remains of a 15th century vessel embedded deep in the sand. Channel 4's 'Time Team' have investigated the site, which is restricted to designated divers. A host of fascinating relics recovered from the wreck can be seen in Teignmouth Museum.

Teignmouth, Whale Bones 1922 73090
A small plaque recording Pike Ward's gift of the whalebones is visible at eye level. The bones show signs of splits and cracks. The arch was removed in 1940 to allow clear sightings for a large gun embedded in the sandstone bank. It survived until about 1950 when it was removed to allotments near the railway line at Broadmeadow. Its remnants were discovered on the council tip years later.

In the 1930s, a wax-moustached gentleman called Mr Shears maintained discipline on the Den and prom. Roller-skaters and other miscreants were treated to a swift clip round the ear! The Salvation Army Band always found favour with local people who gathered to listen to the mellow tones of the instruments.

The prom gained its first wave of decorative lighting in 1934. The Teignmouth Post reported: 'In the 1200 yards strip lighting from the Point to Eastcliff viaduct there are approximately 2000 lamps of red, green, orange, yellow and white. On the grass plots on each side of the pier are two butterfly features each of 160 lamps on poles surmounted by the town's coat of arms... four "trees", two in the grass plot opposite the war memorial and two in

Bottom Left: **Teignmouth
Whale Bones and Promenade 1922** 73091

Top Right: **Teignmouth
The Promenade c1955** T21011
Holidays at British resorts were thriving in the 1940s. Large stacks of deck chairs punctuated the promenade. Ice cream was delivered in aluminium boxes, some can be seen beneath the serving hatch.

Bottom Right: **Teignmouth
Promenade from east 1895** 36852
Here we see the long shadows of early morning with few people about. Gas street lamps were turned on and off individually. Bathing machines (there were 35 at this time) were available on this section of sands, restricted to female use.

Teignmouth, The Parade 1924 76381

In the 1920s, motor transport was still a novelty. Ice cream, tea and shellfish were on sale at refreshment stalls. Thirty minutes boat hire cost a shilling (5p) and anglers found a plentiful supply of bass, pollock, dabs and mackerel. Bunting flutters in the breeze.

front of Courtenay Place... "planted" in tubs with "flowers"... unique. To meet the wishes of the Great Western Railway, in the last span at Eastcliff, red and green lamps are omitted in case it misleads train drivers. The bandstand has 350 lamps of red and yellow. The overall effect from the hotels' frontage is charming.'

The pier opened in 1867 after two years had been spent constructing its 700 foot length at a cost of £8,000. The consulting engineer was Joseph William Wilson - he had already worked on the Crystal Palace and piers at Bognor Regis and Westward Ho! Savouring the salty breezes from the pier was appealing, as was dancing to a string band and concerts by the 1st Rifle Volunteers which took place in a tent at the seaward end. A large pavilion was constructed at the pier head in the 1890s. During its 80 years service, the pavilion had moving picture shows attracting crowds of children to Saturday matinees. Mr Mack

Below:
Teignmouth
Promenade 1936 87484

Twelve years on, and lamps and posts wear necklaces of fairy lights. A new flat-roofed canopy provides shade and shelter. The pier and the Den Pavilion opposite offer abundant entertainment. The Hamiltons, newly built in the style of Swiss chalets, mark the line of the Torquay Road at Shaldon. Redundant bathing machines are lined against the sea wall.

Opposite:
Teignmouth
The Promenade c1955 T21010

The curved wall is a useful landmark for comparisons between this picture and the two previous (see 76381 and 87848). The balustrade-bordered sun deck was supplanted by sea defences constructed in the1970s.

turned the manual cinemagraph, his wife played the piano and their children did a musical turn in the interval. Aside from amusement machines, the pier provided the chance to win prizes, indulge in candy-floss and other tempting confections, take boat trips, try out angling or watch stunt mens' spills, fashion parades and talent contests.

In 1940, a 60-foot section of the pier was cut away as part of anti-invasion measures. Dancing ceased but it was business as usual in the amusement arcade. The post-war pier quickly re-established itself with entertainment and dances. Many a tardy sailor, having missed the liberty boat back to his ship

anchored in the bay, slept instead on the ballroom floor. BBC Radio organists shared the pier bandstand with Evelyn Hardy's all-women resident band. At weekends, 4-500 people paid sixpence to pass through the tollgate halfway down and two shillings to dance the night away in the crowded ballroom. A midnight swim from the shadows under the pier was a special local preserve!

The deteriorating pier was strengthened in 1973 when pile drivers punctured 80 feet of bedrock. Two years later, the ballroom was removed due to severe corrosion in the framework. Continual investment and upgrading by the Brenner family has given the Grand Pier

an optimistic outlook for the new century.

The promenade was selected as the most suitable location for a war memorial in honour of those who lost their lives in World War One. Some 17% of the 600 Teignmouth men and boys who joined the navy were lost, and almost 400 in other armed forces. The troops were supported by a special appeal launched

Teignmouth, Esplanade & Pier 1934 86219

Teignmouth Electric Lighting Company installed the fairy lights that stretch for 1200 yards between the Point and Eastcliff. The first grand switching-on took place on the second Saturday in July 1934. On the left, the new bandstand overlooks the Den, while the jawbone arch and assortment of other whalebones can be seen on the right of the flag staff.

Teignmouth, The Pier 1925 78464

The Duchess of Devonshire pleasure steamer was a frequent caller at the landing stage. In the 1920s it cost one penny to walk the pier's length; 700 feet spanned by arches that once carried gas lamp globes. Concerts, dances and magic lantern shows were staged in the 300-seat pavilion of 1890.

by the Mayoress of Exeter and hundreds of local children were photographed on the Den standing inside huge letters spelling the words 'Forget Me Not Day'. The memorial was erected in 1922. Local stonemasons W H Hayman added the names of those who died in the second conflict to an extension unveiled on Remembrance Sunday 1949.

Teignmouth, Parade 1903 49559

Compare this photograph with that on page 74, divided by half a century and two World Wars. The Edwardians were seldom seen without hats. The pier entrance is smothered with advertisements for whisky, pianos and furniture. Winches for bathing machines stand on the right of the sands and beach tents are also in use.

Left:
**Teignmouth
The Promenade
c1955** T21023

**A more casual style
prevails in 1955.
Now the tower of
St Michael's Church
is more obvious,
following the
destruction of
numbers 1 and 2
Esplanade (the
Berkeley and
Esplanade Hotels)
in September 1942.**

Below:
**Teignmouth
Broken wall
near Lighthouse
1890** 26033B

Above: **Teignmouth, Damaged Wall and Promenade 1890** 26033C

The wall was breached soon after being built. Construction of the lighthouse in 1845 cost the Harbour Commissioners £196.7s. A fort against the French stood nearby a century earlier. Postcard versions of the second image (26033C) sold in great numbers. Storm damage has caused considerable public expenditure on many occasions since.

Opposite: **Teignmouth Boating Pond c1960** T21043

The boating pond's opening in the late 1930s featured the launching of a miniature Golden Hind built by local boatman Pixie Matthews. The pond's elegant balustrades were later replaced by a bland wall. The pier's café ballroom and landing stage are in their final years.

Teignmouth, War Memorial 1922 73083
TUDC considered several options before selecting this location to erect a war memorial in 1922.
It was extended in 1949 to include the losses of World War Two.

Brunel's single-track railway of 1846 swung away from the sea wall before arriving at the station. This was set within a cutting at the centre of a 320-yard long tunnel which penetrated Teignmouth's heartland. Unfortunately, the revolutionary atmospheric system introduced on the broad gauge line was a white elephant of monumental proportions that accounted for a £403,000 write-off. An additional investment of £26,000 allowed for the gargantuan task of opening out the tunnels in the 1880s. People on the platform were henceforth warned by the station porter's loud shout of 'Train be a'comin'!

Increased fares, reduced services, poor connections and tales of rock falls gave the line a poor profile as being expensive, inconvenient, slow and dangerous. By 1890 the situation had improved and the stations of Teignmouth and Dawlish could expect an influx of 4-700 visitors a day. In 1892, an enormous workforce spent a day and a quarter heaving the rails closer together to make the line compatible with the rest of the country's rail network.

In the days of steam, the railway employed a 'Cliff Gang' to carry out scarping of the porous cliffs riddled with springs. A local guidebook paints a picture:

'Tis not the samphire gatherer who plied his giddy trade on the cliffs today but the navvy suspended upon an almost invisible rope ladder, picking at the very soil on which he is

Details from: Left: **Teignmouth, Hole Head 1906** 54070
Right: **Teignmouth, Parade 1896** 37611

suspended'. Even today, walkers on the sea wall occasionally see a handful of men suspended precariously from ropes, clearing loose rocks from the cliff face above the line.

Teignmouth's updated station had platforms of diamond brick beneath glazed cantilevered canopies. New sidings improved handling efficiency of outgoing fish stocks and incoming coal. The grand opening in 1893 coincided with the Duke of York and Princess Mary's wedding day. The town decked itself with bunting and enjoyed a double celebration. A peal of bells rang out and a procession with marching bands wound its way to the Den, where 100 children gathered for a tea party and a commemorative half crown. The momentous day drew to a close with open air dancing and fireworks piercing the night sky with the joyous declaration 'God bless the happy pair'.

By 1905, GWR had re-invented itself into a progressive and successful company. Cheap excursions were snapped up by the working classes enjoying an improved lifestyle. The advent of paid holidays added to the line's increasing impetus, barely stalled by the Great

Teignmouth, Parade 1896 37611
Scenic splendour aside, the cliff-foot route is notorious for frequent disruption caused by the sea's determination to undermine the line. The original broad gauge track of South Devon Railway was narrowed in 1892 to allow the through passage by trains from the Midlands and the North. St Michael's Church and the Esplanade can be seen on the left.

War. An all-time peak was logged in the 1920s. Exeter families packed the so-called Woolworth train, and spent an evening by the sea for a sixpenny fare. Trippers had a taste for brash entertainment and dipped their heads into buckets of flour and ginger to seek out sixpenny pieces. Genteel Victorians were not amused!

Teignmouth, From East Cliff 1903 49555

The scale and design of the fine new bridge of the 1880s with wrought iron lattice girders attracted considerable attention. It gave vehicular access to properties on the railway embankment after the tunnels were removed. At this time, a small shelter stands where, three decades later, the impressive Jubilee Shelter was erected. The large building on the right is Alberta Mansions, the town's first hospital, demolished 1970s.

The holidaymakers failed to arrive in 1939, yet carriage-loads of evacuees and troops did. The line was a vital supply link for Plymouth and, although it was targeted, it never suffered a direct hit. Locals sometimes glimpsed an armoured train passing through as it patrolled between Exeter and Dartmouth on the look-out for E-boats, enemy ships and sea planes.

Increasing car ownership in the 1950s caused a severe decline leading to massive cuts in Devon's railway network. The next decade brought major reductions to services and a huge cultural change. It was the end of the annual summer influx by thousands of visitors travelling the Holiday Line.

**Teignmouth
Hole Head 1906** 54070

The line disappears into Hole Head. Holcombe's headland is dotted with a handful of large properties. Derncleugh House's walled garden slopes towards the wildlife haven of the cliffs of Old Devonian Red Sandstone lining the coast between Dawlish Warren and Torbay. The Parson and Clerk Rocks can be seen at the extremity of the headland.

Two world wars in the 20th century made their mark and Teignmouth's losses are well documented. Both conflicts helped narrow the gulf between the classes, leading indirectly to the conversion of spacious houses into apartments. Without servants, the Georgian and Victorian villas could not easily be kept up as family homes. Plans for post-war Teignmouth were ambitious, but many of the best ideas simply evaporated. Those that materialised led to wholesale demolition that destroyed more character than 79 high explosive bombs dropped by enemy action.

Nevertheless, a renowned local publicist described the nature of 1960s Teignmouth thus: 'She reminds me of a very beautiful gracious aunt, gentle in character and loyal to old

**Teignmouth
The Sands c1955** T21007

Bookings from Exeter to Teignmouth totalled 3000 on August Bank Holiday Monday 1955. The Coast Guard hut stands at the foot of Eastcliff Bridge but the whalebone arch has gone. A café replaces a photographer's studio in the single-storey building on the left. This section of sea wall was replaced by a much higher structure in the 1990s.

**Teignmouth
Parson and Clerk
Rocks 1922** 73093

This walkway, constructed in 1845, was the idea of Admiralty Engineer James Walker, who foresaw its benefit to mariners and fishermen. He hoped it would compensate the public for the loss of other facilities. It is an important resource and part of the long distance South West Way path.

Above: Teignmouth, the Triangle 1922 73096

Skirts and hair were shorter than ever before in the new decade! A two
hour horse-drawn carriage ride for four people cost two shillings (10p).
A Spanish Oak planted as a centrepiece when Victoria became Queen in
1837 was felled to make way for 1920s public lavatories. Electric street
lighting was in its infancy. The Belgian Urn on the Triangle was present-
ed by refugees in recognition of the town's hospitality during the Great
War.

Right: Teignmouth, Bitton Park entrance 1907 58123

Bitton's original 18-acre estate encompassed three large houses
between Clay Lane and Shaldon Bridge. During Lord Exmouth's
occupancy, this house was called Westcliff. TUDC paid £3,300 for it
together with six acres in 1904, and an Isolation Hospital was built just
beyond the west side of the house, where Bitton Court now stands.
At the far end of the road, we can see Mill Lane before development.

friends. Rather staid, frightened of sudden change, fond of children but a little over-awed by her big sister Torquay - the one who always wore flashy jewels.'

Sweeping changes brought about by Local Government reorganisation in 1974 led to the formation of the Town Council beneath the umbrella of Teignbridge District Council. All major resolutions and control of finance were transferred to district level, with the inevitable loss of detailed local knowledge. Railway privatisation, erratic bus timetables and a huge increase in car ownership brought radical change. The town, previously divided by river and railway, was severed for the third time by the construction of the dual carriageway that slithers between three functional housing blocks. Pedestrianisation of the town centre in the 1990s further restricted traffic and affected local business.

More homes are now needed for the local population, 30 per cent higher than a quarter of a century ago (in 1921 a population of 10,976 was recorded, in 1969 it was 12,260, by 2001 this had risen to 15,013). Experts, poised to prepare a detailed study of the town, may suggest a suitable location for additional housing. The land below the railway line cannot be expanded other than by packing the community into unacceptably high levels. Proposals for major alterations excite vociferous response and decisions often fail to gain favour. The first decade of the 21st century will embrace many interesting challenges, and bids for greater funding may secure finance for acceptable improvement.

A great deal of respectful therapy based on an intimate knowledge of Teignmouth's heartbeat is needed if she is to be maintained as a beautiful and buoyant place.

Teignmouth c1965 T21096

The prominent workshop and sheds of Morgan Giles' shipyard are seen at the end of a period spanning 44 years. The yard's demise coincided with the last decade of significant holiday trade. The visual tour through Teignmouth has come full circle for a last, lingering look at the gem of south Devon.

BIBLIOGRAPHY

Black's Guide 1868

Brabner's Gazeteer 1895

Book of Teignmouth - Beatrix Cresswell

History of Teignmouth - Grace Griffiths

Homelands Guide 1906

Exeter-Newton Abbot, A Railway History - Peter Kay

Rails along the Sea Wall - Peter Kay

Teignmouth in Old Picture Postcards Volume 1 - Ann Pearson

Visitor's guide to Teignmouth - Ann Pearson

Piggott's Directory 1836

Story of the Riviera Cinema - Peter D Prince

Ship's Monthly magazine 1996

Teignmouth Journal 1875

Teignmouth Post & Gazette

Ward Lock & Co Red Guide 1920s

The Western Times

Burton's Bounty - Viv Wilson

Herald Express Teignmouth Talk columns 1990 to 2001 - Viv Wilson

Teignmouth in Old Picture Postcards Volume 2 - Viv Wilson

Frith Book Co Titles

www.francisfrith.co.uk

The Frith Book Company publishes over 100 new titles each year. A selection of those currently available are listed below. For latest catalogue please contact Frith Book Co.

Town Books 96 pages, approx 100 photos. County and Themed Books 128 pages, approx 150 photos (unless specified). All titles hardback laminated case and jacket except those indicated pb (paperback)

Amersham, Chesham & Rickmansworth (pb)			Dartmoor	1-85937-145-0	£14.99
	1-85937-340-2	£9.99	Derby (pb)	1-85937-367-4	£9.99
Ancient Monuments & Stone Circles	1-85937-143-4	£17.99	Derbyshire (pb)	1-85937-196-5	£9.99
Aylesbury (pb)	1-85937-227-9	£9.99	Devon (pb)	1-85937-297-x	£9.99
Bakewell	1-85937-113-2	£12.99	Dorset (pb)	1-85937-269-4	£9.99
Barnstaple (pb)	1-85937-300-3	£9.99	Dorset Churches	1-85937-172-8	£17.99
Bath (pb)	1-85937419-0	£9.99	Dorset Coast (pb)	1-85937-299-6	£9.99
Bedford (pb)	1-85937-205-8	£9.99	Dorset Living Memories	1-85937-210-4	£14.99
Berkshire (pb)	1-85937-191-4	£9.99	Down the Severn	1-85937-118-3	£14.99
Berkshire Churches	1-85937-170-1	£17.99	Down the Thames (pb)	1-85937-278-3	£9.99
Blackpool (pb)	1-85937-382-8	£9.99	Down the Trent	1-85937-311-9	£14.99
Bognor Regis (pb)	1-85937-431-x	£9.99	Dublin (pb)	1-85937-231-7	£9.99
Bournemouth	1-85937-067-5	£12.99	East Anglia (pb)	1-85937-265-1	£9.99
Bradford (pb)	1-85937-204-x	£9.99	East London	1-85937-080-2	£14.99
Brighton & Hove(pb)	1-85937-192-2	£8.99	East Sussex	1-85937-130-2	£14.99
Bristol (pb)	1-85937-264-3	£9.99	Eastbourne	1-85937-061-6	£12.99
British Life A Century Ago (pb)	1-85937-213-9	£9.99	Edinburgh (pb)	1-85937-193-0	£8.99
Buckinghamshire (pb)	1-85937-200-7	£9.99	England in the 1880s	1-85937-331-3	£17.99
Camberley (pb)	1-85937-222-8	£9.99	English Castles (pb)	1-85937-434-4	£9.99
Cambridge (pb)	1-85937-422-0	£9.99	English Country Houses	1-85937-161-2	£17.99
Cambridgeshire (pb)	1-85937-420-4	£9.99	Essex (pb)	1-85937-270-8	£9.99
Canals & Waterways (pb)	1-85937-291-0	£9.99	Exeter	1-85937-126-4	£12.99
Canterbury Cathedral (pb)	1-85937-179-5	£9.99	Exmoor	1-85937-132-9	£14.99
Cardiff (pb)	1-85937-093-4	£9.99	Falmouth	1-85937-066-7	£12.99
Carmarthenshire	1-85937-216-3	£14.99	Folkestone (pb)	1-85937-124-8	£9.99
Chelmsford (pb)	1-85937-310-0	£9.99	Glasgow (pb)	1-85937-190-6	£9.99
Cheltenham (pb)	1-85937-095-0	£9.99	Gloucestershire	1-85937-102-7	£14.99
Cheshire (pb)	1-85937-271-6	£9.99	Great Yarmouth (pb)	1-85937-426-3	£9.99
Chester	1-85937-090-x	£12.99	Greater Manchester (pb)	1-85937-266-x	£9.99
Chesterfield	1-85937-378-x	£9.99	Guildford (pb)	1-85937-410-7	£9.99
Chichester (pb)	1-85937-228-7	£9.99	Hampshire (pb)	1-85937-279-1	£9.99
Colchester (pb)	1-85937-188-4	£8.99	Hampshire Churches (pb)	1-85937-207-4	£9.99
Cornish Coast	1-85937-163-9	£14.99	Harrogate	1-85937-423-9	£9.99
Cornwall (pb)	1-85937-229-5	£9.99	Hastings & Bexhill (pb)	1-85937-131-0	£9.99
Cornwall Living Memories	1-85937-248-1	£14.99	Heart of Lancashire (pb)	1-85937-197-3	£9.99
Cotswolds (pb)	1-85937-230-9	£9.99	Helston (pb)	1-85937-214-7	£9.99
Cotswolds Living Memories	1-85937-255-4	£14.99	Hereford (pb)	1-85937-175-2	£9.99
County Durham	1-85937-123-x	£14.99	Herefordshire	1-85937-174-4	£14.99
Croydon Living Memories	1-85937-162-0	£9.99	Hertfordshire (pb)	1-85937-247-3	£9.99
Cumbria	1-85937-101-9	£14.99	Horsham (pb)	1-85937-432-8	£9.99

Available from your local bookshop or from the publisher

Humberside	1-85937-215-5	£14.99	St Albans (pb)	1-85937-341-0	£9.99
Hythe, Romney Marsh & Ashford	1-85937-256-2	£9.99	St Ives (pb)	1-85937415-8	£9.99
Ipswich (pb)	1-85937-424-7	£9.99	Scotland (pb)	1-85937-182-5	£9.99
Ireland (pb)	1-85937-181-7	£9.99	Scottish Castles (pb)	1-85937-323-2	£9.99
Isle of Man (pb)	1-85937-268-6	£9.99	Sevenoaks & Tunbridge	1-85937-057-8	£12.99
Isles of Scilly	1-85937-136-1	£14.99	Sheffield, South Yorks (pb)	1-85937-267-8	£9.99
Isle of Wight (pb)	1-85937-429-8	£9.99	Shrewsbury (pb)	1-85937-325-9	£9.99
Isle of Wight Living Memories	1-85937-304-6	£14.99	Shropshire (pb)	1-85937-326-7	£9.99
Kent (pb)	1-85937-189-2	£9.99	Somerset	1-85937-153-1	£14.99
Kent Living Memories	1-85937-125-6	£14.99	South Devon Coast	1-85937-107-8	£14.99
Lake District (pb)	1-85937-275-9	£9.99	South Devon Living Memories	1-85937-168-x	£14.99
Lancaster, Morecambe & Heysham (pb)	1-85937-233-3	£9.99	South Hams	1-85937-220-1	£14.99
Leeds (pb)	1-85937-202-3	£9.99	Southampton (pb)	1-85937-427-1	£9.99
Leicester	1-85937-073-x	£12.99	Southport (pb)	1-85937-425-5	£9.99
Leicestershire (pb)	1-85937-185-x	£9.99	Staffordshire	1-85937-047-0	£12.99
Lincolnshire (pb)	1-85937-433-6	£9.99	Stratford upon Avon	1-85937-098-5	£12.99
Liverpool & Merseyside (pb)	1-85937-234-1	£9.99	Suffolk (pb)	1-85937-221-x	£9.99
London (pb)	1-85937-183-3	£9.99	Suffolk Coast	1-85937-259-7	£14.99
Ludlow (pb)	1-85937-176-0	£9.99	Surrey (pb)	1-85937-240-6	£9.99
Luton (pb)	1-85937-235-x	£9.99	Sussex (pb)	1-85937-184-1	£9.99
Maidstone	1-85937-056-x	£14.99	Swansea (pb)	1-85937-167-1	£9.99
Manchester (pb)	1-85937-198-1	£9.99	Tees Valley & Cleveland	1-85937-211-2	£14.99
Middlesex	1-85937-158-2	£14.99	Thanet (pb)	1-85937-116-7	£9.99
New Forest	1-85937-128-0	£14.99	Tiverton (pb)	1-85937-178-7	£9.99
Newark (pb)	1-85937-366-6	£9.99	Torbay	1-85937-063-2	£12.99
Newport, Wales (pb)	1-85937-258-9	£9.99	Truro	1-85937-147-7	£12.99
Newquay (pb)	1-85937-421-2	£9.99	Victorian and Edwardian Cornwall	1-85937-252-x	£14.99
Norfolk (pb)	1-85937-195-7	£9.99	Victorian & Edwardian Devon	1-85937-253-8	£14.99
Norfolk Living Memories	1-85937-217-1	£14.99	Victorian & Edwardian Kent	1-85937-149-3	£14.99
Northamptonshire	1-85937-150-7	£14.99	Vic & Ed Maritime Album	1-85937-144-2	£17.99
Northumberland Tyne & Wear (pb)	1-85937-281-3	£9.99	Victorian and Edwardian Sussex	1-85937-157-4	£14.99
North Devon Coast	1-85937-146-9	£14.99	Victorian & Edwardian Yorkshire	1-85937-154-x	£14.99
North Devon Living Memories	1-85937-261-9	£14.99	Victorian Seaside	1-85937-159-0	£17.99
North London	1-85937-206-6	£14.99	Villages of Devon (pb)	1-85937-293-7	£9.99
North Wales (pb)	1-85937-298-8	£9.99	Villages of Kent (pb)	1-85937-294-5	£9.99
North Yorkshire (pb)	1-85937-236-8	£9.99	Villages of Sussex (pb)	1-85937-295-3	£9.99
Norwich (pb)	1-85937-194-9	£8.99	Warwickshire (pb)	1-85937-203-1	£9.99
Nottingham (pb)	1-85937-324-0	£9.99	Welsh Castles (pb)	1-85937-322-4	£9.99
Nottinghamshire (pb)	1-85937-187-6	£9.99	West Midlands (pb)	1-85937-289-9	£9.99
Oxford (pb)	1-85937-411-5	£9.99	West Sussex	1-85937-148-5	£14.99
Oxfordshire (pb)	1-85937-430-1	£9.99	West Yorkshire (pb)	1-85937-201-5	£9.99
Peak District (pb)	1-85937-280-5	£9.99	Weymouth (pb)	1-85937-209-0	£9.99
Penzance	1-85937-069-1	£12.99	Wiltshire (pb)	1-85937-277-5	£9.99
Peterborough (pb)	1-85937-219-8	£9.99	Wiltshire Churches (pb)	1-85937-171-x	£9.99
Piers	1-85937-237-6	£17.99	Wiltshire Living Memories	1-85937-245-7	£14.99
Plymouth	1-85937-119-1	£12.99	Winchester (pb)	1-85937-428-x	£9.99
Poole & Sandbanks (pb)	1-85937-251-1	£9.99	Windmills & Watermills	1-85937-242-2	£17.99
Preston (pb)	1-85937-212-0	£9.99	Worcester (pb)	1-85937-165-5	£9.99
Reading (pb)	1-85937-238-4	£9.99	Worcestershire	1-85937-152-3	£14.99
Romford (pb)	1-85937-319-4	£9.99	York (pb)	1-85937-199-x	£9.99
Salisbury (pb)	1-85937-239-2	£9.99	Yorkshire (pb)	1-85937-186-8	£9.99
Scarborough (pb)	1-85937-379-8	£9.99	Yorkshire Living Memories	1-85937-166-3	£14.99

See Frith books on the internet www.francisfrith.co.uk

Francis Frith would doubtless be pleased to know that the pioneering publishing venture he started in 1860 still continues today. A hundred and forty years later, The Francis Frith Collection continues in the same innovative tradition and is now one of the foremost publishers of vintage photographs in the world. Some of the current activities include:

Interior Decoration

Today Frith's photographs can be seen framed and as giant wall murals in thousands of pubs, restaurants, hotels, banks, retail stores and other public buildings throughout the country. In every case they enhance the unique local atmosphere of the places they depict and provide reminders of gentler days in an increasingly busy and frenetic world.

Product Promotions

Frith products are used by many major companies to promote the sales of their own products or to reinforce their own history and heritage. Frith promotions have been used by Hovis bread, Courage beers, Scots Porage Oats, Colman's mustard, Cadbury's foods, Mellow Birds coffee, Dunhill pipe tobacco, Guinness, and Bulmer's Cider.

Genealogy and Family History

As the interest in family history and roots grows world-wide, more and more people are turning to Frith's photographs of Great Britain for images of the towns, villages and streets where their ancestors lived; and, of course, photographs of the churches and chapels where their ancestors were christened, married and buried are an essential part of every genealogy tree and family album.

Frith Products

All Frith photographs are available Framed or just as Mounted Prints and Posters (size 23 x 16 inches). These may be ordered from the address below. From time to time other products - Address Books, Calendars, Table Mats, etc - are available.

The Internet

Already twenty thousand Frith photographs can be viewed and purchased on the internet through the Frith websites and a myriad of partner sites.

For more detailed information on Frith companies and products, look at these sites:

www.francisfrith.co.uk
www.francisfrith.com
(for North American visitors)

See the complete list of Frith Books at:

www.francisfrith.co.uk

This web site is regularly updated with the latest list of publications from the Frith Book Company. If you wish to buy books relating to another part of the country that your local bookshop does not stock, you may purchase on-line.

For further information, trade, or author enquiries please contact us at the address below:
The Francis Frith Collection, Frith's Barn, Teffont, Salisbury, Wiltshire, England SP3 5QP.
Tel: +44 (0)1722 716 376 Fax: +44 (0)1722 716 881 Email: sales@francisfrith.co.uk

---

See Frith books on the internet www.francisfrith.co.uk